SURVIVING
YOUR
BABY & CHILD

SURVIVING YOUR BABY & CHILD

Victor Langer

Illustrated by Jackie Hurd
(except pages 78-83
illustrated by Erika Langer)

Collier Books
Macmillan Publishing Company
New York

Collier Macmillan Publishers
London

C

Collier Books
Macmillan Publishing Company
866 Third Avenue, New York, NY 10022
Collier Macmillan Canada, Inc.

Book design and mechanicals: Victor Langer

Library of Congress Cataloging-in-Publication Data

Langer, Victor.
    Surviving your baby & child/Victor Langer: illustrated by Jackie Hurd and Erika Langer.
        p.   cm.
    ISBN 0-02-077221-1
    1. Child rearing. I. Title. II. Title: Surviving your baby and child.
HQ769.L238 1989
649.1–dc19   88-31318
                                                                  CIP

Macmillan books are available at special discounts for bulk purchases for sales promotions, premiums, fund-raising, or educational use. For details contact:

        Special Sales Director
        Macmillan Publishing Company
        866 Third Avenue
        New York, NY 10022

10 9 8 7 6 5 4 3 2 1

Printed in the United States of America

For Erika

Contents

Introduction

As a new or prospective parent you may have heard horror stories from other parents about what an ordeal it is to raise a child. You may have read books describing all the hard work, sacrifice and difficulty. You may have thought, "It can't be that bad." It is.

If you have the point of view that creating a baby is the most creative thing you can do, you may find later that you have created a monster.

Or you may not know what to expect. Expect the worst.

The task that lies before you will take everything you've got. And keep on taking.

This is not to say that it won't also be rewarding. Your baby and child will thrill you, if he doesn't kill you. So it comes down to a question of *survival*. And survival is a question of endurance and knowledge.

The more you get to know Baby, the more you know what you're up against. And the more Baby gets to know you, the more he knows what he can get away with.

Don't count on love to get you through. Love is good, but shrewdness is more important. Don't let Baby walk all over you. Don't be afraid to stand up to Baby and put your foot down. Remember, Baby is out for number one. That cuteness is just a trick.

Trust your instincts. Your first instinct is to survive; next comes caring for your child.

And don't think too far ahead. Just try to make it through the first five years. Good luck.

Part One

**Difficult
Beginnings**

Mother's View–
Father's View

Mother's and Father's points of view of a new baby may differ widely. Be aware of these differences, acknowledge them and try to reconcile them.

Mother's View	Father's View
A lifetime of love.	Help with the harvest.
The miracle of a new life.	A new tax exemption.
The ecstasy of birth.	Stretch marks.
The music of a little voice lilting through the house.	Good-bye, peace and quiet.
The fun of watching them play.	Trashed-out house.
The pleasure of comforting distress.	Sleepless nights.
Constant companionship.	A ball and chain.
The thrill of watching them grow.	Growing expense and responsibility.
The satisfaction of accommodating baby's schedule.	Good-bye, spontaneous sex.

Equipment You Will Need

Recent advances in design of equipment for infants and young children has made parenting a lot easier. Here are some of the essentials:

SuperStroller

A high-performance stroller for today's malls. With telescoping ramming-bumpers for crowded conditions. Hazard light for wetness or fumes. Tamper-proof parking brake. Embossed windshield hides fingerprints; front and rear wiper.

Quality Timer

A timer for "quality time." Set for ten minutes (new parents) or fifteen minutes (experienced parents). When the bell sounds you know that quality time is over, and everyone can go back to being normal.

Maximum-Security Playpen

Baby serves his time so you can take your time. Reinforced Mylar sides hold up if baby tries to make a break for it. Sensitive alarm sounds if he tries to go over the top. Tough ripstop nylon bottom keeps baby from tunneling out.

The Tot Tub

This hot tub and whirlpool baby-bath goes one step beyond the Leboyer hot bath for after delivery. Also great for soothing the older child stressed-out after a day of peer-group pressure.

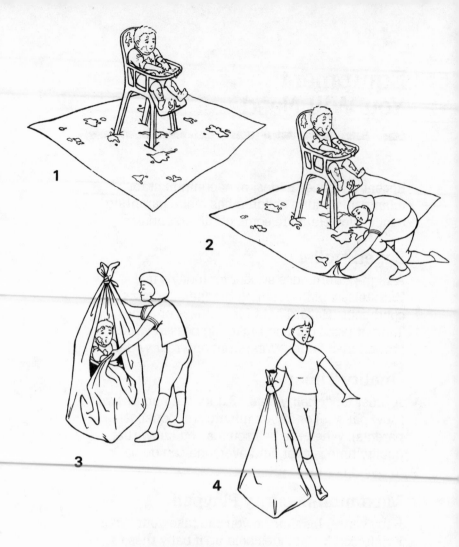

Disposable High-Chair

An ingenious solution to the problem of wide-spread dinner debris. Biodegradable cardboard high-chair is surrounded by 8-foot-square no-leak drop-cloth. After the feeding frenzy just pick up the four corners of the dropcloth, bring together over the top of the high chair, secure with a twist-tie and dispose of like any trash bag.

The Do-not Donut

This inflated walker looks like a giant chocolate-covered donut. Keeps trouble just out of arm's reach. Makes for mobility without mess. Baby can *go*, and *look*, but not *do*. Inflated design will not damage guests.

Juke Potty

A musical potty-chair that plays many selections, not just the traditional "How Dry I Am." Titles include "It's Now or Never," "Stormy Weather," "Anticipation," "Baby, I Can't Wait Forever" and "Bridge Over Troubled Water."

"Rock-a-Byte Baby" Computer Cradle

Start programming early. Powerful yet gentle microprocessor, padded keyboard and extra soft software fit right in with baby. Unit plays cry-activated video lullabies. Effectively structures quiet-alert time.

Upwardly Mobile Mobile

A crib mobile to start baby thinking about the time when he will have to make the switch from parental bonds to tax-sheltered bonds. Four dangling objects highly researched for appeal: Rolled-up *Wall Street Journal*, hand-held printing calculator, monogrammed lobster pick and mobile phone.

Upscale Baby Scale

Premium scale for weighing-in of the baby who is a real contender. Digital readout in both English and metric for the world-class child.

Concealed Breast Pump

Dual-intake low-profile unit may be worn all day under clothing. No one will know. Express yourself whenever you need to, anytime, anywhere. Milk drains through hidden tubes into pouch in pocket or purse.

Laundry Pitchfork

An ordinary pitchfork is the fastest way to move very large piles of laundry from place to place.

Laser Diaper Vaporizer

Compact high-powered laser disintegrates dirty diapers without a trace. No more laundering of dirty diapers or collecting them for the diaper service. No more bulky disposables cluttering up the trash.

Crybaby Muffler

Sound-muffling headphones worn by parent allow parent to tune out baby. Effective noise-deadening design of the type used on aircraft carrier decks. Variable setting allows you to hear a little, or nothing. Set for "Whimper," "Cry," "Scream," or "Oblivion."

"No-Peek–No-Leak" Nursing Bra

Nurse in privacy in public places. Easy-open Velcro cups flip down and pneumatically deploy mini privacy screen stored within, much like auto air bags. After nursing, screen folds back into cups. Neoprene cup gaskets put an end to embarrassing leaks.

"The No-Nuke" Self-Destructing Pacifier

Ingenious pacifier dissolves completely over a period of several weeks, helping child to gently kick the habit.

Toydozer

Bulldozer-type sit-and-ride child's room cleaner.
Cuts a swath 36 inches wide through toys and
clutter. Compacts clutter in neat stacks around
the perimeter of the room. Mulcher attachment
allows for quick disposal of old, broken or
unwanted toys. Not recommended for operation
by child.

Toddler Magnet

When your toddler gives you the slip in a
crowded store, just turn on this powerful electro-
magnet, and he comes sliding back. More
discreet than a harness and leash. (Child must
wear chain-mail vest, not included.)

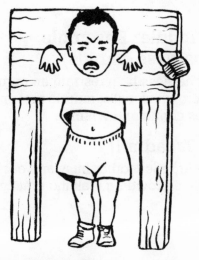

Preschooler Pillory

When all else fails, immobilize a wild preschooler with a pillory. Authentic medieval design still works well. Also a perfect restrainer for splinter removal.

Shoe Marble-Guard

Marbles all over the floor are a real hazard. Unit fits around edge of shoe and brushes away marbles before you slip on them.

Artwork Shredder

Many children produce a prodigious amount of artwork. But often nine out of ten pieces are not worth saving. How do you deal with the clutter? If you just throw out a picture, all too often it's reclaimed from the trash by hurt and angry child. The answer is an artwork shredder. All that clutter just vanishes overnight without a trace.

Canine Toddler Ensemble
(leash, harness, muzzle)

Leash and harness help restrain an unruly toddler in crowded malls, muzzle prevents biting and muffles crying and whining.

Toddler Treadmill

Keep an energetic toddler busy and out of trouble, while providing walking practice.

Girls versus Boys

Some parents prefer a girl and some a boy. Each is wonderful in her/his own way. A girl and a boy each has her/his own special charm, but she/he manifests it differently. Notice the different ways she/he expresses her/himself depending on whether she/he is a girl, and/or whether he/she is a boy.

Girl	Boy
Kisses and hugs	Headlocks and noogies
Plays dress-up	Plays shoot-'em-up
Favorite toy: doll	Favorite toy: monsters
Nature appreciation: picks flowers	Nature appreciation: picks wings off butterflies
Ballet	Karate
Watercolor painting	Spatter painting
Bubble bath	Mud bath
Sand castle	Sand bombs
Wants to be when grows up: nurse, ballerina, vet	Wants to be when grows up: wrecker, samurai, robot
Swims with friends	Dunks and splashes friends
Bracelets	Handcuffs
Skipping with friends	Tripping friends
Graceful skating	Speed skating
Sparklers	Firecrackers
Plays piano	Takes piano apart
Favorite color: pink	Favorite color: Khaki camouflage
Favorite food: chicken chunks	Favorite food: Gummy Worms
Taunts and teases	Punches and kicks

Basic Training for Prospective Parents

During pregnancy don't just sit around and wait for the baby. There's plenty you can do to get ready for the grueling days ahead. Soon many new and taxing demands, both mental and physical, will be made upon you. Prepare yourself with these simple exercises:

- Read it again: Read a children's book, such as "Chicken Little," aloud five times. Repeat three times daily.

- Play it again: Get a music box that plays one simple tune, such as "Twinkle,Twinkle Little Star," and listen to it twenty-five times in succession. Repeat four times daily.

- Interruption torture: Learn to take constant interruption in your stride. Get an alarm watch and set it to go off at ten-minute intervals all day.

- Spell it: Have your spouse ask you to spell words she wants to write down. See if you can keep going for an hour and a half, twice a day.

- Counting torture: Make an audiotape of someone counting up to ninety-nine. Play fifteen times. Rest. Repeat.

- Practice running an obstacle course to improve your speed and agility so that you will be able to catch your 4-year-old in a crowded mall.

- Soon you will be doing familiar things from unfamiliar angles. Improve your manual dexterity by doing things to another person that you normally do only to yourself, such as brushing teeth, combing hair, tying shoes, and dressing and undressing. Practice on any unwilling person. Subject should squirm throughout.

- One-hand handicap: While holding a 10-pound doll in one arm, practice doing things with only one free hand: Open a child-resistant aspirin bottle, make Cream of Wheat, clean the bathtub, vacuum, knead bread, etc.

- Marathon Card Game: Play Go Fish with spouse for two hours. Then switch to Slapjack for two hours. Rest. Repeat.

- Have your spouse ask you "Why?" every time you say anything, however matter-of-fact, throughout the day.

- Make paper chains for four hours. Then switch to jigsaw puzzles for four hours.

- Have your spouse rise an hour before you in the morning. Then, as soon as you awake, and while you are still groggy, have her/him assault you with cheerful and animated conversation and questions.

- Practice talking on the phone with very loud background noise, such as a video movie with lots of shouting and laughing, with volume turned way up.

Getting to Know You

Your newborn baby will be a stranger at first. Give yourself time to get used to a new face around the house. Soon you will be able to determine your baby's needs by subtle differences in facial expression:

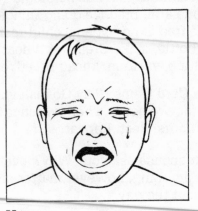

Hungry

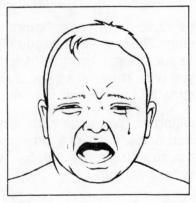

Wet

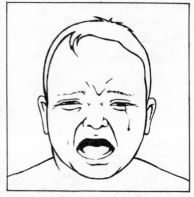

Lonely

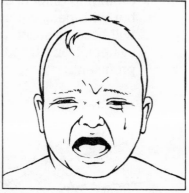

Tired

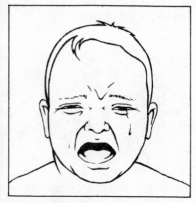

Upset Tummy

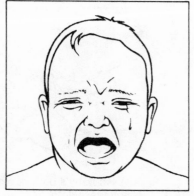

Fever

Diapering Made Simple

Changing diapers is a formidable task at first, but with perseverance it can be mastered and will become second nature. Follow this proven system. Don't try to improvise until you are proficient.

1. Raise baby's legs and remove old diaper. If baby is only wet, wipe with damp washcloth, and skip steps 2-5.

2. If baby is soiled, get as much as you can with diaper, then deposit diaper in toilet to get rid of unwanted house guests.

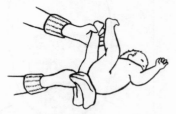

3. Wash baby's bottom with soapy washcloth.

4. Rinse out washcloth, soap up again, and carefully clean within all skin folds. If baby is a boy, wear swimming goggles to protect eyes.

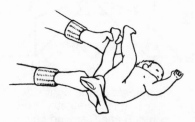

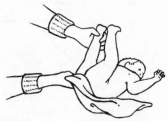

5. With a second damp wash-cloth rinse baby thoroughly to remove irritating soap film.

6. Dry baby completely with soft toweling or a blow dryer.

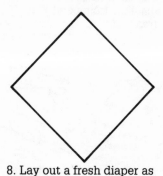

7. Apply baby oil, powder, and zinc oxide ointment if diaper rash is present.

8. Lay out a fresh diaper as shown.

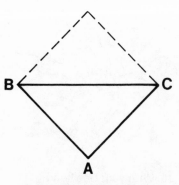

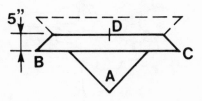

9. Fold diaper in half diagonally for a double thickness.

10. Fold the diagonal line B-C over and down to form a top band about 5" deep.

27

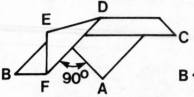

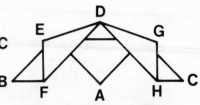

11. Now, starting at the top center point D, fold down the left side of the top band so that the line D-F intersects the line E-A at right angles and about half the distance from point E as from point A.

12. Repeat on the right side, checking for symmetry. End points B and C should be equidistant from an imaginary horizontal drawn through point A.

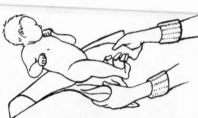

13. Align baby over diaper. Central axis A-D of diaper should be congruent with baby's spine, with top point D about 3" above navel.

14. Bring point A up between baby's legs and flatten down onto his stomach.

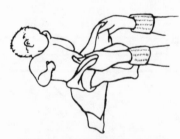

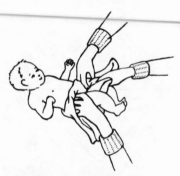

15. Bring waistband left endpoint B up and over, positioning over point A. Hold both points in place.

16. With your free hand swing right band endpoint C over into position near endpoint B.

17. While holding all four layers together, check crotch for snugness.

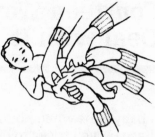

18. Without releasing tab C, slip safety pin through all layers at a point midway between B and C.

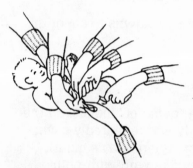

19. Now release tension from tab C while still pressing down at point G.

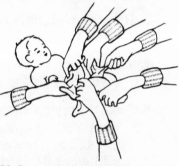

20. Insert a second safety pin to secure tab B to flap G-H.

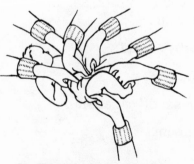

21. Check for snugness all around, especially at leg openings. If not snug repeat steps 15-21.

Crying–
Fourteen Ways to
Deal with It

If baby cries when nothing obvious is wrong, try these proven tricks to deal with crying:

1. Make your spouse deal with it.

2. Play audiotape of whale songs.

3. Hire troop of professional clowns to cheer up baby.

4. Take baby on roller coaster. Repeat until crying subsides.

5. Make the crying into a "game"of "Indians-on-the-Warpath" by quickly and repeatedly covering and uncovering crying baby's mouth with your hand to make wuh-wuh-wuh sound.

6. Try tickling baby.

7. Don't let baby know you are upset. Set an example by acting calm.

8. Break an egg over baby's head.

9. Set off a smoke alarm.

10. Place baby in car and set off car alarm.

11. Lock yourself in bathroom.

12. Place baby on his back and lay a cold wet washcloth over his face. (Remember to remove after three minutes.)

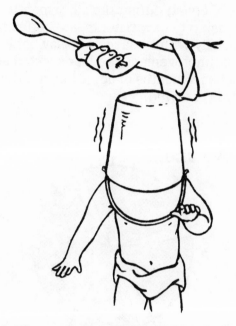

13. Place a large metal pail over baby's head and bang repeatedly with metal cooking spoon.

14. Place a large metal pail over *your* head and bang repeatedly with metal cooking spoon.

If baby still cries, it means that you are simply a bad parent and nothing can be done about it.

Cycles
of
Crying

Long periods of crying during the early months—
though distressing to new parents—are perfectly
normal, especially with a colicky or fussy baby.
But significant improvement can be expected as
baby approaches 6 months of age. Here are the
typical patterns of crying:

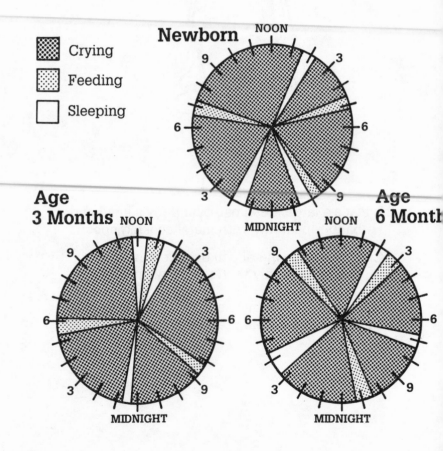

A Balanced Diet

Proper diet is the key factor in health and growth. Be willing to accommodate your child's personal taste preferences, but be sure he gets a balance of the six essential foodstuffs.

Vegetables provide most necessary vitamins and minerals, as well as roughage for proper digestion. In addition, root vegetables, such as the mashed potatoes shown here, provide carbohydrates.

Meats and Fish are needed as a primary source of highest quality protein and fatty acids, plus vitamins A and D.

Eggs are a good secondary source of protein, and supply vitamin D and iron as well.

Fruits are rich in vitamins A, B and C. Raw fruits are preferable to highly processed ones.

Grains are the staple carbohydrate fuel to supply your child's high energy needs.

Milk Products are the best all-around foods. They contain protein, fat and calcium vital for bones.

Skillful Sleeping

Adequate sleep is essential for parents in order for them to cope with full and demanding days. But all too often, interrupted sleep is the rule. To minimize lost sleep train yourself to get back to sleep as quickly as possible after an interruption, and don't waste precious minutes on anger or self-pity. In the scenario shown below, total lost sleep may be as little as a half hour.

11:00 P.M. Mother and father retire after a hard day. They are looking forward to a few moments of intimacy. As matters begin to reach a crescendo . . .

11:18 P.M. Child cries. She has wet her bed massively. Mother goes in, changes bed and child.

36

12:03 A.M. Mother returns to parents' room. Father is now asleep. She collapses and sleeps.

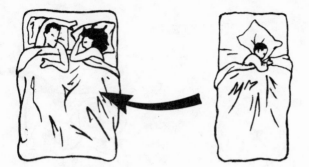

1:12 A.M. Child cries. She is thirsty. Father stumbles in with water.

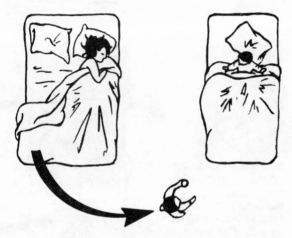

2:19 A.M. Child staggers into parents' room, crying, waking them both. She is having bad dreams. She gets in bed with them.

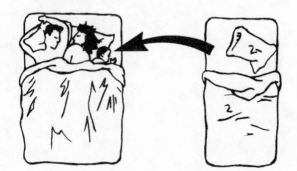

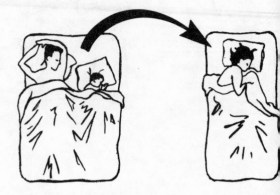

3:37 A.M. Mother feels crowded between father and child, goes into child's bed.

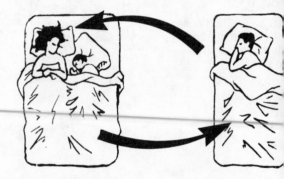

4:06 A.M. Child wakes, crying for mother for unknown reason, waking both parents. Mother returns to parents' bed, father goes into child's bed.

5:42 A.M. Sleeping child keeps kicking mother, waking her. Mother returns to child's bed, now also occupied by father.

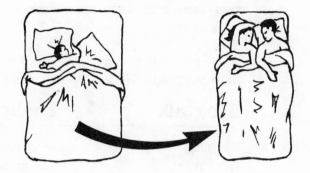

6:45 A.M. Alarm clock sounds in parents' room, waking and frightening child.

Glossary of Baby Talk

Babies can tell you a great deal if you can speak their language. Here's a basic vocabulary:

Baby talk	English
Nim-nim!	Feed me!
Kah-kah!	Change me!
Mm-bah!	Hold me!
Nn-kih-doo!	Put me down!
Huh-huh-nih!	Turn me over!
Nkah-kih-nih!	Sit me up!
Mmmmm-buh!	Burp me!
Wah-wah-soo	Bathe me!
Wah-nih-no!	Walk me!
Mmnah-lih-lih-nnkoh-kee.	Get that cigarette out of here, please.
Diedee-wah-wah.	This diaper is leaking.
Hah-yoo-jaja-mih.	These jammies are killing me.
Dah-dah-kah-ee?	Why is Daddy crying?
Mah-koh-nuh-kih-bah-huh.	Mommy don't doze off—Baby wants to play.
Yuk-yuk-ooluh-nih-ptah!	Strained liver again!
Kee-kee-kee-kee!	Smoke alarm.
Noo-hah-yuk-yuk-fff.	Back off with the bad breath please.
Bah-hnih-tah-koo-lah-lah.	I broke camera. Buy new one.
Bah-ruh-ruh-kih-nih-bah-lih.	I spilled again. See pretty ink on rug.
Bah-rrrooh-kee-reeow-nih!	I squeeze kitty. Kitty scratch.

Safety
First

The world is bristling with hazards for your baby or child. Learn to spot them and take preventive measures:

- Turn all dressers to the wall to keep little hands from pulling heavy drawers all the way out.

- Staple chicken wire to the fronts of bookcases to keep a toddler from pulling items over on his head.

- Keep chain saws well out of reach.

- Discard old ice picks and meat hooks.

- Cover all wells, swimming pools, open elevator shafts, sinkholes and meteor craters.

- Store barbed wire well away from play areas.

- Bracket all lamps to tables and tables to floors.

- Do not allow tarantulas near the crib of a very young child.

- Never breast-feed during an earthquake.

- Cover all sliding glass doors with indoor-outdoor carpet.

- Keep at least 30 feet from child operating a jackhammer.

- Teach your child not to play:
    within 50 yards of arc welding.
    within 100 yards of limestone quarries.
    within 200 yards of open-hearth steel mills.
    within 500 yards of oil drilling rigs.
    within 100 miles of a subatomic particle accelerator.
    within 300 miles of a thermonuclear weapons testing area.
    within 10 light years of a supernova.

A Workout with Baby

Just because you have a newborn baby doesn't mean your body has to go to pot. Even though baby is a workout *you* can still work out . . . . just work baby in. Think of baby as an extra challenge, like ankle or wrist weights. Many exercises will lend themselves to baby's participation.

- Aerobic walking. A perfect exercise to practice with a fussy newborn. Brisk walking comforts baby and gives you a workout. Don't hold baby; use a carrier so you can swing your arms.

- Push-ups. With baby on your back, do half the usual number.

- Sit-ups while breast-feeding. With baby resting on your chest, do twenty-five, then switch breasts.

- Jogging, pushing baby in stroller. Sure to put a cranky baby to sleep. Use heavy-duty stroller.

- Pumping iron. Substitute baby for barbell. Baby will love it. Give a newborn fifty overhead lifts, twenty-five for a 6-month-old.

- Jumping jacks. Baby does his own, alongside you, in his suspended jumper-seat.

- Thigh-trimming horsie ride. While seated, bounce baby 100 times on each leg. Not after baby has just eaten.

An Album
of Firsts

Keep a photo album of important "firsts" along the way. This will give you a sense of the passage of time and remind you that each phase of growth will not last forever, that eventually you *will* make it through those furious first five years.

First
Tantrum

First
aerobic
Workout

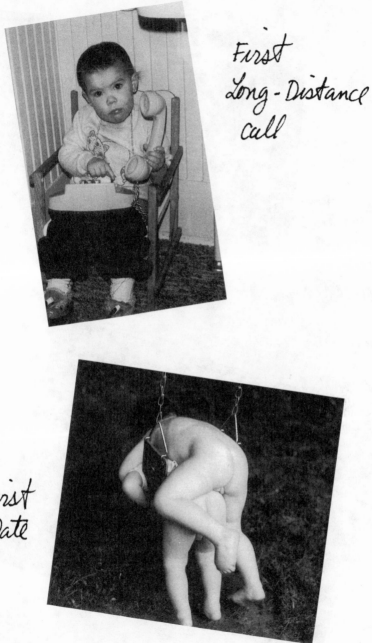

First
Long-Distance
Call

First
Date

First
Board
meeting

First
moon
Landing

First
BMW

First
Computer

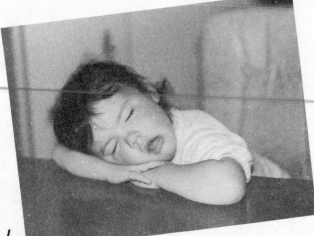

First
Investment
(Collectibles)

First
Political
Convention

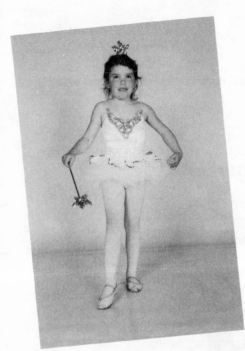

First
Academy
Award

First
Press
Conference

Growth Tables

▬▶ ▬▶ ▬▶ ▬▶ ▬▶ ▬▶ ▬▶ ▬▶ ▬▶

Each stage of growth holds new wonder for both child and parent. Here are some of the highlights to look for, tabulated by age and type of skill.

The First 12 Months

Physical

Able to pull self up to sitting position, with help of your hair.

Overturns jar of buttons to explore effect of gravity.

Sucks on doorknobs, light switches and other protuberances around the house.

Imitates sound of parents arguing.

May swallow jewelry.

Able to hold crystal candlestick in each hand. May bang together.

Bangs playfully with spoon at own reflection in antique mirror.

Mental

Knows that candy you have just hidden has not actually ceased to exist.

Plays with new toy for up to twenty seconds.

Social

Allows mother to leave room for up to ten seconds.

Able to distinguish between mother's face and chimpanzee's.

Bites without warning.

May coo or gurgle briefly when not crying.

Age 1

Able to crawl to the edge of cliffs and dams.
Can raise arms high enough to dump cereal over
    own head.
Able to clear entire table by pulling self up on
    tablecloth.
Drools less.
Can stand upright briefly by holding onto lace
    curtain.
Can carry up to three eggs in cupped hands.

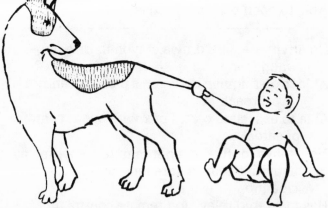

Hands growing stronger. Able to firmly grasp
    tail of neighbor's dog.
Now spills beverages less than five times daily.

Explores in-out relationship of objects with
    antique vase.
Stops crying for at least ten minutes at a time.
Attention span for quiet play increases to thirty
    seconds.

Bites with warning.

Age 2

Physical

Able to reach and open medicine chest.

Now strong enough to pull a Chippendale end
table over on self.

Eye-hand coordination improves; repeatedly un-
ties shoelaces of all family members.

Manual dexterity increases; using spoon as a
lever, is now able to fling food up to 25 feet.
(Not a rigid standard—your child's actual
distance may vary.)

Able to build tower of three to four china teacups.

Able to open perfume bottles.

Mental

Creativity begins; draws crayon murals on
wallpaper.

Able to distinguish between a piece of candy and
a cockroach.

Able to associate cereal box with sugar content
of cereal.

Now plays for five to eight minutes at a time at
activities that require lengthy setup and
cleanup.

Has mastered television remote control unit.

Has reached 40 percent of computer literacy.

Social

Allows mother to leave room for up to fifteen
seconds.

Ages 3 and 4

Physical

Able to run with lolly in mouth.
Can walk and chew gum at the same time.
Able to leap tall buildings at a single bound.

Mental

Can write own name on sofa with chocolate
  pudding.
Has reached 60 percent level of computer
  literacy.
Now able to watch television for up to five hours
  without dozing off.
Able to operate VCR (except for auto-record
  mode).
Able to microwave own frozen dinner.
Able to release parking brake of car.

Social

Begins to say "I hate you" when angry.
Shows interest in tasks. Helps with houseclean-
  ing by sponge-mopping furniture.
Starts requesting money.
Cheats at checkers.

Miscellaneous Tips

- Remove chewing gum from a child's hair by ironing hair on low setting. Gum will stick to iron. Remove from iron with vinegar and a wire brush. Remove from wire brush with propane torch.

- Tie a cowbell around toddler's neck when he hides from you in a store.

- Keep baby from unrolling the toilet paper by storing the paper inside toilet tank. Set the roll on the little float to keep it dry.

- Prevent baby from locking self in bathroom by keeping an empty potato sack draped over top of door.

- Apply petroleum jelly to all doorknobs in the house to keep baby from opening doors.

- When burping baby, drape an empty potato sack over your shoulder. (If you don't have a spare, use the one that's draped over the bathroom door.)

- Keep fighting siblings apart by chaining them to their beds.

- When a newborn's umbilical cord stub falls off a few days after birth, save it and have it cast in bronze for a mantelpiece keepsake or Christmas tree ornament.

- Telephone tug-of-war: Keep a toddler from pulling on the phone cord while you're on the phone by wrapping the excess around your neck.

- When you have two kids in bunkbeds and one is a bedwetter, put the bedwetter on the *bottom* bunk to avoid a "leaky roof" and *two* beds to change instead of one.

- When breastfeeding, keep track of which breast you used last by attaching a helium balloon to the bra strap on the *other* side. Next feeding, start with the breast with the balloon.

- Great decorating tip: Make an unusual and nostalgic collage on one wall of child's room using old bills, invoices and receipts from the hospital, obstetrician, pediatrician, dentist, children's store, diaper service, etc.

- Keep an infant's sharp little fingernails from scratching your face by wearing a skier's knit face mask when you poke your head into his crib to greet him.

- Get rid of a security blanket by cutting a small piece off it every day, so that the child doesn't notice. When it becomes as small as a napkin it will no longer provide security and the child will discard it by himself.

- Teach fairness with money by setting an example. If you borrow from your child's birthday money or savings account, be sure to pay it back with interest at a rate at least equal to the prevailing prime rate. (A kiss does not count as interest.)

- When shopping in a supermarket with a young child in the cart, keep him from clearing the shelves by using colorful yarn to tie his hands together behind his back.

- Teach politeness by always being polite to the child, not just in front of company: "*Please* take your feet off my magazine . . . *Thanks* for not wetting again last night . . . *May I* have my glasses back now? . . . *I apologize* for screaming in your face before."

- Make a "tantrum chamber" from an empty closet, for a child to work it out alone. Provide a light, and padded walls (use old quilts) for soundproofing and injury prevention.

- Curtail telephone abuse by little girls. Make them set a timer every time they use the phone. Set a limit of five hours per day.

- A sure cure for thumbsucking: Have all family members suck their thumbs for two weeks to show the child how silly it looks.

- A large stain of permanent marker on light colored wall-to-wall carpet can be camouflaged by tie-dyeing the carpet.

- Hide an indelible stain of grape juice on the wall by hanging up some child's colorful artwork over the spot.

- Curb nail-biting by sticking an olive on every finger.

- Ease the jealousy of a very devoted dog when a new baby arrives home by letting him nurse along with baby. This will also help him to bond with baby.

- Keep a roll of paper towels on your belt for quick cleanups during the day.

- If tension and frustration for parent build up to unbearable level, simply go into a closet and scream for fifteen to thirty seconds. (Use child's "Tantrum Chamber" if not occupied.) Soothe throat afterward with herbal tea and honey.

- Bent plastic place mats can easily be flattened out again by taking them out to the driveway and running them over several times with the car.

- Spray baby with Pam for easier dressing, especially with tight jammies.

- Keep houseplants in closets to avoid damage by toddlers.

- Prevent tooth marks on the edges of tables during teething by painting the edges of all tables with vinegar. It won't hurt the finish and it will discourage little mouths from latching on.

- Prevent an infant from unzipping his own jammies during the night by putting them on backward.

Part Two

Light
at the End
of the Tunnel

Embarrassing Questions

One of the great charms of children is their fresh approach to the mysteries of existence. But this may put an adult in an embarrassing position when he has to come up with a prompt and plausible retort to a question on religion, sex or magic. Be ready to think fast. Here are some suggested answers to keep in mind for a few of the most common questions.

How can Santa be at two malls at the same time?
- Those are Santa's brothers.
- Santa beat us to this mall because his reindeer can fly over the traffic.
- Santa beat us to this mall because they let him use the handicapped parking spaces.

Why is Tippy climbing up on Ginger's back?
- Ginger is giving Tippy a horsie ride.
- Tippy is telling her a secret.
- Let's go inside now.

What does the Tooth Fairy do with the teeth?
- I don't know, dear. The Tooth Fairy is not a nonprofit organization, so she doesn't have to tell us what she does with the teeth.
- She shines them up and comes back again when you're asleep and plants them in your mouth again, and they grow into your big grown-up teeth.
- She turns them into dental hygienists.

Where will I be when I die?
- Where are you now?
- In heaven, with God, Santa and Barbie.
- In dog food, if you're not good.

Why did the wicked Queen want to eat Snow White's lung and liver?
- Because this is the original story and not the sanitized version.
- Because she needed protein.
- Because she was a sadistic maniac.

Why did God make the Red Sea open up to let the Hebrews go across?
- Because the Hebrews had good contacts.
- It's not our place to know the will of God.
- Because if he didn't, he wouldn't have the Hebrews to kick around anymore.

Why did all the dinosaurs die?
- They didn't – there's one under your bed.
- Because they didn't finish up all their red meat.
- Because they were playing too close to an asteroid collision.

Discipline

In most cases, today's streetwise preschooler will respond to gentle persuasion by laughing in your face. Many years of excessive and misguided permissiveness have produced a crop of spoiled-rotten brats. Parents have had enough. Now we are witnessing a widespread backlash. Parents realize now that firmness is indispensable. Unconsciously, the child wants the parent to set limits. He doesn't want mush for a mom or a doormat for a dad. So don't feel guilty. It's for their own good. Be firm with impunity.

- Don't procrastinate with punishment. Strike while the iron is hot.

- Give a clear ultimatum. Don't say "When you do that, it makes Mommy sad." Say "If you do that again you're dead meat!!!"

- Get personal. Don't be abstract. Don't be above name-calling. Don't say "That's inappropriate behavior." Say "You are a selfish, spoiled-rotten, ungrateful little brat!!!"

- Threats should have teeth. Don't make idle threats you can't back up, such as "I'm going to call the garbagemen to come and take you to the dump."

- Know the basics of wrestling and karate.

Chart of Offenses and Recommended Punishments

Offense	Punishment
Assault and Battery:	
Minor: Throwing sand, pushing, spitting	No TV for ten days, with possible appeal to other parent
Major: Biting, kicking, punching	No TV for ten days, with no chance of appeal (Includes video movies.)
Malicious Mischief:	
Graffiti, exterior	Hard labor – cleaning up own room
Graffiti, interior	Solitary confinement: Go to own room for two hours, with possibility of parole in fifteen minutes
Disturbing the Peace: Door-slamming, loud kazoo, party noisemaker, etc.	Broccoli three nights in a row
Illegal Parking (third offense): Tricycle in front of garage door	Five days no dessert
Breaking and Entering: (Entering Mommy's bedroom and breaking perfume bottle, etc.)	No use of telephone, ten days (Effective only with girls.)
Miscellaneous Misdemeanors:	
Bed-wetting	Pillory, two hours
Unauthorized flower picking	No computer games, two hours
Littering	50¢ fine or fifteen minutes confined to own room
Loitering (dawdling when called for dinner)	No gum, five days
Indecent exposure	No snacks between between-meal-snacks, two days
Petty Larceny (theft of sibling's squeeze toy)	Forfeit toy of equal value
Grand Larceny (theft and mis-placement of Mommy's keys)	Pillory, three hours

Stain Removal Guide

With a child on the scene, little accidents are inevitable. Get used to them. Remember, the price of a perfect house is an inhibited child. There can be stain without pain—if you know the secrets of stain removal.

Stain	Object	Remedy
Urine	Velvet sofa	Apply paste of baking soda. Rinse. Blot. Flood with ammonia solution. Blot.
Drool	Suede jacket	Soak in lemon juice. Wring out.
Stool	White satin blouse	Soak in bleach. Wring hands.
Eggie	Rayon skirt	Soak in vinegar. Wring neck.
Peanut butter	Deep shag carpeting	Cover stain with kerosene. Set aflame. Let burn five seconds. Blow out. Vacuum charred area.
Squashed frog	Leather car seat	Remove with putty knife. Blot.
Squashed goldfish	Black mink coat	Gnash teeth, cover body with sackcloth.
Crayon	Silk lamp shade	Sandblast, then soak in sulfuric acid.
Play-Doh, soft	Brocade tablecloth	Cover with cornstarch. Let stand overnight. Hose down.
Play-Doh, hardened	Flocked wallpaper	Dab with clear nail polish. When dry, flick off.
Unidentified green matter	Antique tapestry	Remove with salad tongs. Rub with hard cheese.
Unidentified yellow matter	Oriental rug	Rub with an onion.

Mealtime Negotiation

When it comes to eating foods that are good for him, but which he may not like, today's toddler drives a hard bargain. You can't expect him to make all gone simply by insisting loudly. You have to offer him something in return. Apply the subtle strategies of negotiation to achieve your ends. But make sure he doesn't get the best of *you*. For most effective bargaining use these guidelines for equivalent values of main course foods and dessert rewards.

Food Item	Dessert Reward
Three more bites of liver	= Two Oreos
Two more bites of liver and one bite of potato	= Popsicle or Fudgsicle
One more bite of liver, one bite of potato and one bite of peas	= Two Fig Newtons
All of your broccoli	= Three vanilla wafers
Half of your milk	= Chocolate-frosted cream filled cupcake
All of your milk	= Two Gummy Bears or Two Gummy Worms
Two more bites of eggie	= Slurpie
Just one more fish stick	= Blow Pop and two pieces of squirting gum
Half of your creamed spinach	= Fruit Roll-Up and two jawbreakers
The last two beets	= Aerosol whipped cream dispensed directly into mouth for three seconds
Just one of your Brussels sprouts	= Aerosol whipped cream dispensed directly into mouth for six seconds

Bedtime Rituals

Rituals mean a lot to a young child, especially at bedtime, a time fraught with anxiety over separation, the dark, monsters, dreams, etc. An elaborate bedtime ritual may be tiresome to an adult, but it is better than an hour and a half of screaming. But know where to draw the line. A desperate child will go for all he can get. Ritual should not exceed forty-five minutes.

1. Warm bath.
2. Jammies on.
3. Brush teeth, peepee.
4. Read three books.
5. Read one more book.
6. Read just one more book.
7. Walk around house, kiss and say good night to all family members, including all pets.
8. Enter child's room. Check carefully for dinosaurs, especially under furniture, to child's complete satisfaction.
9. Kiss all twenty-six stuffed animals good night. (Parent must kiss all too.)
10. Select three favorite stuffed animals to sleep with.
11. Turn on night-light to scare away gremlins, goblins, ghouls and ghosts.
12. Rearrange all furnishings and clothing to eliminate any threatening looking shadows.
13. Wind up lullaby music box.
14. Sprinkle "magic" baby powder around room to keep trolls away.

15. Kiss, cover and tuck in three favorite stuffed animals.
16. Kiss, cover and tuck in child.
17. Rock for ten minutes.
18. Pat back for ten minutes.
19. Rewind music box.
20. One more kiss.
21. Leave quietly.
22. Leave door open amount specified by child.
23. Leave hall light on.
24. Turn radio on in an adjoining room so that child is reassured that Mommy and Daddy are near.
25. Pray.
26. If grumbling sets in and persists for over twenty minutes, repeat steps 13 to 25.

Homemade Fun & Games

To entertain your child/children you need not spend a fortune on manufactured toys and games, many of which will have a short life span. With a little imagination there's no limit to the number of things you can make or improvise.

- **Stepping-Stone Cushions**: Make a "river" of aluminum foil, running through the living room, and put down furniture cushions for "stepping stones" for the kids to try to get across.

- **Ladder-Back Chairs Climbing Gym**: A set of antique ladder-back chairs can make a great rainy-day climbing gym. Make different configurations by lining them up, stacking them or overturning them.

- **Paper-Towel Cores**: Never throw these away. They have uses as a telescope, kaleidoscope, pretend laser weapon, lunar probe soil sampler, unicorn horn, worm tunnel, pretend Geiger counter, etc.

- **Animal Tracks**: Kids cut old flip-flops in the shapes of different animal footprints, then step into finger paint and make animal tracks around the house.

- **Four-poster "Clubhouse"**: Turn an antique four-poster bed into an instant clubhouse by draping an old painting drop cloth over it.

- **Window Ant Farm**: A fascinating ant farm can easily be made by filling the space between a window and storm window with dirt. Add ants, and voilà.

- **Candy Fishing (four or more)**: A sofa makes a perfect "boat" if you take the seat cushions off and stand them up along the front. To make a "pond" turn the coffee table upside down and put an oval mirror in it. Kids sit in the boat and try to catch candy-bar "fish" with fishing rods equipped with chewing-gum "hooks."

- **Panty-Hose Python Puppets**: A pair of panty-hose makes a pair of perfect python puppets for a puppet presentation.

- **Snail Trail Hide-and-Seek (three or more)**:
  Catch a snail and let it go in the house. All
  kids cover their eyes for five minutes, then
  see who can find the snail first by following
  the slime trail. If you accidentally step on
  the snail, you're out of the game.

- **Beanbag-Chair Bayonet Charge (for boys)**: Let
  kids play commando to their hearts' content
  with meat skewers and an old beanbag
  chair.

- **Pillow-Fight Feather-Mural (two or more)**:
  Kids "paint" a mural with glue on a wall
  covered with washable wallpaper. Then
  they have a pillow fight with feather pil-
  lows. When the feathers settle, you have a
  feather mural.

- **Chandelier Swing**: Turn a chandelier into a
  rainy-day swing. Tie a length of nylon rope
  to one of the arms. Pass the other end
  through a hole made in a pie tin, which will
  serve as the seat, and knot it.

- **Elephant House**: Child makes an "elephant"
  out of the house. The "trunk" is a 10-foot-
  long piece of clothes-dryer vent hose draped
  out of a second-story window. "Tusks"are
  two skis, each sticking out of a lower-story
  window.

- **Toilet-Paper Streamers for Bike**: Put a roll of
  toilet paper on the end of each handlebar.
  Unroll about 4 feet for a great streamer.
  When tattered, tear off and unroll more.

- **Baby-Tooth Bracelet**: Instead of giving baby teeth to the Tooth Fairy, save them to make a fun and unusual bracelet. Ask Daddy to drill holes in them and string them on dental floss.

- **Living-Room Hockey Court**: A living room with hardwood floor can become an instant hockey court for rainy-day fun. An over-turned love seat at the end of the room makes a perfect goal. Brass andirons serve as hockey sticks, and a marble ashtray can be used as the puck. Kids "skate" in their socks on the slippery floor.

- **Take It Apart (for boys)**: You can entertain a boy for hours by giving him something he can take apart:

Typewriter	2 hours
Sewing machine	3 hours
Crystal Chandelier	4 hours
Antique grandfather clock	6 hours

- **Cockroach Collection (for boys)**: Boys love to collect urban wildlife. After your young entomologist has amassed a large collection, have him paint his specimens with clear nail polish to preserve them, glue little magnets to their underbellies, and display the entire collection on the frig door. (Also good as memo holders.)

- **Trampoline Chair**: A Victorian wing chair makes a perfect trampoline. Its coil springs are bouncier than modern foam-rubber furniture.

- **Snow White (for a girl)**: Girl lies on her back on the floor under a glass coffee table pretending to be Snow White lying in her glass coffin under the Wicked Queen's spell. Stuffed animals can be the Seven Dwarfs standing around her. Most girls will stay under the spell for up to half an hour, thus giving parent a nice break.

Store-Bought Fun & Games

The selection at the toy store is staggering, and while there are many unwholesome choices, quite a few are worthwhile. Here are some of our favorites from this year's crop:

- **"Smooth-Operator" Surgery Set**: Goes beyond the traditional "playing doctor" with mere routine checkups. Provides hands-on experience treating a lifelike pretend patient. Instructions for twelve operations, from an easy tonsillectomy to a tricky kidney transplant. Includes gowns, masks, gloves, scalpels, clamps, sponges, sutures, pretend blood and donor organs.

- **"Spoiled Brat on Board" Car Sign**: Display sign on car and drive around town to publicly embarrass a child who has misbehaved.

- **Rocking Stegosaurus**: Give child the real feel of a prehistoric pony ride.

- **Pollution Set**: Teaches principles of ecology. Make a mess of home environment and then clean it up. Includes pretend oil slick, airborne ash flakes, glow-in-the-dark pretend nuclear waste.

- **Programmable Parent Doll**: Does everything parent does: reads stories, comforts, scolds and threatens. Rechargeable after worn out at end of every day. Gives real parent a break.

- **"Lady Leaks-a-Lot" Doll**: Lifelike doll cries real tears, drools, sweats, throws up and peepees. You never know when. Gives child realistic parenting experience.

- **"Doctor Gross" Gross-out Kit**: Child turns into mad scientist who formulates goop, glop, sludge, slop, scum and ooze to gross out parents and friends. Nontoxic.

- **"Feedback" Teaching Machine**: Machine dispenses snack when child gives the right answer. Language and math program. Effective learning experience, especially with a hungry child. Shows them that they have to compete to eat.

- **Bath Piranha**: Lifelike bath toy swims and clicks teeth. Gets a dawdler out of the tub fast.

- **Garbage-Collecting Set**: The new collecting sensation for the child tired of collecting shells, rocks, leaves and baseball cards. Scale-model city dump, garbage truck, bull-dozer, and plenty of pretend garbage, gulls and rats.

- **Ghostbusters Slime Gun**: Slime your opponent before he slimes you. Shoots harmless but disgusting pellets of slime.

- **Baby's Baby's Baby**: Just as every girl wants a baby doll, she knows that her baby wants a baby, and so on. Hence this three-generation baby-doll set.

Understanding Children's Art

Having to ask "What is it?" embarrasses the parent and insults the child. With a little practice you can figure out even the most garbled composition. There are only a few basic themes, such as security, anxiety, exploration and fascination. Here is a representative sampling.

My House
Crayon on linen pillowcase
16" x 28"

Mommy Loves Me
Finger paint on embroidered tablecloth
32" x 47"

Daddy Is Mad
Egg tempera on lace curtain
35" x 45"

A Day at the Beach
Permanent marker on refrigerator door
40" x 65"

Dinosaurs Fighting
Grape jelly on velour cushion
15" x 22"

My Room
Acrylic on braided rug
18" x 27"

Car Trip Tips

Car trips with kids can be trying or traumatic. Here are some tips to help smooth out the bumps by being creative with car games and smart about logistics.

- Count dead animals on the road. Score 4 points for skunks, 3 points for raccoons, 2 points for opossums and 1 point for unidentifiable.

- Count how many times Daddy gets mad at other drivers.

- A game for siblings: Count how many times each kid says "When will we be there?" The one who says it most by the end of the trip loses.

- Let the kids "shoot" the drivers of other cars, but only from behind so as not to startle them.

- Watch for the odometer to be all one number. (But no crowding the driver!)

- For a backseat driver make a pretend gearshift from a Tootsie-Roll Pop (wrapped) stuck in a wad of Play-Doh.

- Smear hand cream on a window and let kids "finger paint."

- Make a sunroof kite from an old road map, some sticks and string.

- If siblings are fighting over a toy, threaten to throw it out the window. If that doesn't work, pull over and blow the horn until they stop.

- Stop at rest areas often to sweep crumbs out of the car and mop up spills, to prevent cockroach infestation.

- If you run out of drinks between rest areas, pull over and let child suck on the windshield washer squirter.

- Keep an infant's bottle warm by taping it to the engine block.

- Keep a toddler from unlocking his door by strapping his arms to his sides under his seat belt.

Thank-you Notes

Thank-you notes need not be a chore. Make them into a creative exercise. Have your child compose his own notes. Remind him to praise the gift, and encourage him to be natural and sincere.

Dear Aunt Dee, Uncle Ed, Sarah, Molly, Patrick, Tippy and Ginger,
    Thank you for the pencil box for my burthday. Mommy says how cheep can you get? I like to put my pencils in it and then take them out. And I like to open and close it and listen to the little click it makes.
        Mommy said to write I love you,
            Jason

Dear Mr. Wilson,

Thank you for the very nice money for Chrismas. Daddy took it away to save it for me in his pocket. When I grow up I want to be big and fat just like you. I like the way your red cheeks wiggle when you eat, just like Santa. Daddy says to be nice to you cause you're the Boss. Don't be too bossy or you won't have any freinds.

Your freind,
Jason Murphy

Dear Aunty O, Uncle Bob, Tim
   and Terry,
      Thank you for the
Space Battlestation.
I haven't broken it yet,
egsept for the laser
sattelite-killer part. Mommy
said what a innerpropriate
gift— what does that mean?
I'm sorry that I spilled the
pretend alien's blood on
Aunty O's pretty dress, Mommy
said it serves her right.

         I love you,
            Jason

Dear Gramma and Grampa,
Thank you for the
Incredible Hulk. I put
it with my 3 other
Incredible Hulks. I had
fun with you at the zoo
when I ran away and
you chased me and then
Grampa got mad. Can I come
and vizit soon and bring
my guiney pigs and my frog?
Daddy said he would like
that too.   I Love you,
Jason

Dear Aunt Bee and Uncle Joe,
   Thank you for the drum
set. I play it all the time.
Mommy says its driveing
her crasy. I miss you.

Aunt Bee — when you
kissed me goodbye your
mustash tickled me.

Mommy said you stayed
too long. Come and stay
with us again soon for
too long.

                    Love,   X X X
                    Jason   o O o

Test
Yourself

Parenting can be puzzling. See if you have all the answers.

1. What is the worst fear of most children?

   ☐ A. TV malfunction
   ☐ B. Out of ketchup
   ☐ C. Security blanket in laundry
   ☐ D. Hungry tyrannosaurus
   ☐ E. Going down the drain

2. What is the worst fear of most parents?

   ☐ A. Cavities
   ☐ B. Putting eye out
   ☐ C. Cracking head open
   ☐ D. Child throwing tantrum in public
   ☐ E. Parent throwing tantrum in public

3. Which of these doesn't belong?

   ☐ A. Meconium
   ☐ B. Diarrhea
   ☐ C. Projectile vomiting
   ☐ D. Nasal syringe

4. Which of these characters is most admired by 4-year-old girls?

   ☐ A. Snow White
   ☐ B. Cinderella
   ☐ C. Sleeping Beauty
   ☐ D. Mom
   ☐ E. Barbie

5. Which of these mystical superheroes is most admired by 4-year-old boys?

   ☐ A. Easter Bunny
   ☐ B. Tooth Fairy
   ☐ C. Santa
   ☐ D. God
   ☐ E. The Incredible Hulk

6. What is the favorite pet of 4-year-old boys?

   ☐ A. Mole rat
   ☐ B. Salamander
   ☐ C. Dung beetle
   ☐ D. Banana slug

7. What is the best way to handle a tantrum in public?

   ☐ A. Laugh and point at the child, and get others to gather around and do the same
   ☐ B. Immediately walk away from child so that no one suspects that you are the parent
   ☐ C. Stuff a spare diaper in his mouth
   ☐ D. Immediately give in to whatever it was the child wanted

8. What is the favorite brand of breakfast cereal of 3–4-year-olds?

   ☐ A. Command-O's (tiny sugar-coated terrorists)
   ☐ B. Phrosted Phobias (sugar-frosted scary demons)
   ☐ C. Sugorillas (sugar-coated apes)
   ☐ D. Dental Chex (low sugar)

9. What is the most coveted toy among 4-year-old girls?

- ☐ A. Barbie Ice Cream Shoppe set
- ☐ B. Barbie Malibu Beach Party
- ☐ C. Barbie Ferrari
- ☐ D. Barbie Dream Kitchen
- ☐ E. Barbie Townhouse

10. What is the most coveted toy among 4-year-old boys?

- ☐ A. G.I. Joe Laser Battle Game
- ☐ B. G.I. Joe Marauder Motorcycle Tank
- ☐ C. G.I. Joe Phantom X-19 Stealth Fighter
- ☐ D. G.I. Joe "Charbroil"Flamethrower
- ☐ E. G.I. Joe Vindicator Hovercraft

11. What is the most important thing to look for in a baby-sitter?

- ☐ A. Takes instructions
- ☐ B. Takes MasterCard
- ☐ C. Calls child "dude"
- ☐ D. Nose ring
- ☐ E. Bloodshot eyes

Answers: 1.C, 2.E, 3.D, 4.E, 5.E, 6.A, 7.A, 8.B, 9.A, 10.A, 11.B

93

The Perfect Preschooler

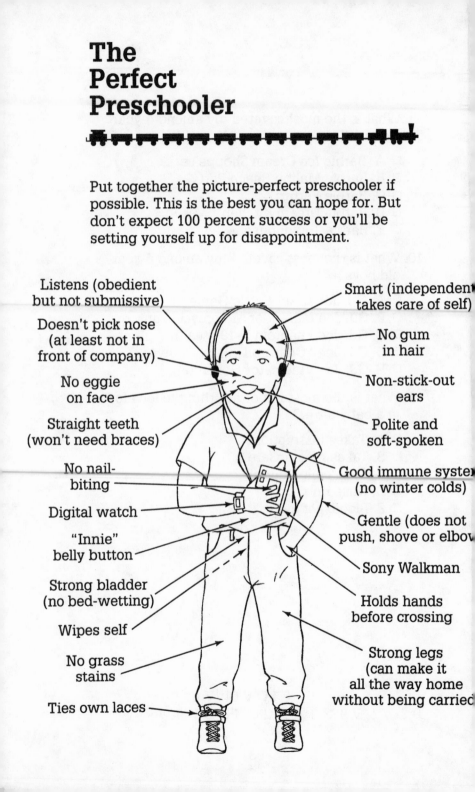

Put together the picture-perfect preschooler if possible. This is the best you can hope for. But don't expect 100 percent success or you'll be setting yourself up for disappointment.

Listens (obedient but not submissive)

Doesn't pick nose (at least not in front of company)

No eggie on face

Straight teeth (won't need braces)

No nail-biting

Digital watch

"Innie" belly button

Strong bladder (no bed-wetting)

Wipes self

No grass stains

Ties own laces

Smart (independent takes care of self)

No gum in hair

Non-stick-out ears

Polite and soft-spoken

Good immune system (no winter colds)

Gentle (does not push, shove or elbow

Sony Walkman

Holds hands before crossing

Strong legs (can make it all the way home without being carried

Thank you
Madeleine,
Philip
and
Walter.